DREAMER CODE

A Bridge Between Dream Exploration and Real-World Innovation

Brian D Mckee

Brian D Mckee

CONTENTS

INTRODUCTION

Dreams, Innovation, Cultivating Creativity and Nurturing an Entrepreneurial Mindset

Welcome to a journey of inspiration, growth, and transformation! In the pages that lie ahead, we will go on a quest to unlock the immense potential within each of us, being empowered to become catalysts of change, champions of innovation, and beacons of creativity. I am excited to be your guide on this adventure, sharing with you some valuable insights and experiences common among innovators as well as ones that have shaped my own path.

Allow me to introduce myself. I am Brian McKee, entrepreneur, cybersecurity professional, graphic designer, dreamer and pastor of City of Light Church, nestled in the heart of Southeastern WI —the most ethnically segregated region in the United States. My passion for community engagement and my unwavering belief in the power of creativity have led me on a remarkable journey of discovery and purpose.

This book will have a mixture of spiritual, entrepreneurial and innovation focused themes. I invite you to keep an open mind as you may encounter some concepts that may be new or out of your normal realm of thinking. I will do my best to share an evidence-based approach to how I arrived at what I believe will be some impactful solutions to everyday challenges you may face as the reader.

As I write this book, we are 4 years removed from a Global pandemic, while staring one of the worst global economic crises in decades square in the face.

In these uncertain times, as our world faces unprecedented challenges, we find ourselves standing at a crossroads. It is precisely during these moments of adversity that pure survival challenges us to summon our courage, embrace innovation, and nurture our inherent creativity to come out of this season on top. We must foster an entrepreneurial mindset that enables us to not only adapt to change but also shape our own destinies.

History records that during tough times, necessity breaks way to ingenuity. God-inspired dreams and visions present possibilities that we couldn't come up with on our own. People are willing to take risks to test theories that they may have been too afraid to try when life was comfortable. If you are up for the challenge to learn and try new things to release some of the pressure you are facing in life right now, this book is for you.

Throughout the early 2020's, I witnessed firsthand the incredible potential for transformation that lies within individuals and communities. When faced with the disruptive force of a global pandemic, my team and I were determined to pivot, adapt, and find creative solutions to keep our church thriving and the community we serve filled with hope.

Recognizing the immense talent within our multiethnic/multicultural congregation, we offered artists and creatives a platform to showcase their gifts through engaging video content. By partnering with struggling local businesses, we not only provided them with much-needed exposure but also highlighted their essential role in the fabric of our community. Sunday streamed events in their establishments became a bridge, connecting the spirit of worship with the heart of our community.

But our efforts did not stop there. We sought to nourish the soul and promote positive mental health by hosting family BBQ-style gatherings in local outdoor venues throughout the summer. These gatherings served as a source of joy, connection, and rejuvenation for our community during a time of isolation and uncertainty.

Inspired by the belief that true change requires collective action, we reached out to local leaders from over 100 churches across denominations, businesses and community organizations. In these crucial conversations, we confronted the deep wounds of racial division, fostering understanding, healing, and unity. Together, we took steps to advocate for changes in local law enforcement practices, striving to build a safer and more equitable community for all.

As we embark on this journey together, I am excited to share with you the lessons I have learned, the stories that have shaped me, and the wisdom that has emerged from these transformative experiences. We will explore the essential principles of innovation, creativity, dream interpretation and the entrepreneurial mindset, drawing inspiration from a diverse range of sources—both contemporary and timeless.

Through engaging narratives, practical exercises, and profound insights, we will delve into the power of thinking differently, challenging assumptions, embracing failure, fostering collaboration, and harnessing the iterative process. We will also uncover the remarkable wisdom found within ancient texts, highlighting the stories of individuals who experienced divine insight through dreams and visions.

So, my friends, let us embark on this transformative journey together. Let us embrace the possibilities that lie within us and tap into the reservoirs of innovation, creativity, and entrepreneurial spirit. As we unlock our potential, we will not only shape our own destinies but also inspire positive change in our communities and the world.

The path ahead may not always be easy, but with faith, determination, and a spirit of adventure, we will overcome obstacles, seize opportunities, and emerge as catalysts for innovation, champions of creativity, and pioneers of entrepreneurial endeavors. I invite you to join me as we embark on this life-transforming expedition.

Are you ready to unleash the boundless power within? Let's embark on this journey together, for we are destined to soar to new heights of innovation, creativity, and entrepreneurial greatness!

Chapter 1 awaits, where we will explore the fundamental principles of thinking differently, unlocking the creative genius within, and embracing a mindset that defies limits. Get ready to embark on a transformational experience that will leave an indelible mark on your life and the lives of those around you.

Together, let us cultivate innovation, nurture creativity, and ignite the entrepreneurial fire within to solve some of the largest challenges we face in life!

CHAPTER 1: THE SONS OF ISSACHAR:

Discerning Times and Seasons for Innovation and Entrepreneurship

The captivating story of the Sons of Issachar is the vantage point from which we will begin unlocking the code of understanding cultural, social and global landscapes, with an idea of how to develop meaningful strategy to find solutions to everyday needs.

The Sons of Issachar were an ancient Biblical tribe known for their exceptional understanding of times and seasons. They did not just know what season they were in, but they understood how to leverage its characteristics to solve the problems they faced.

We will unravel their ancestry, explore instances where they displayed wisdom in overcoming challenges, and examine the profound meaning of discerning times and seasons as mentioned in 1 Chronicles 12 in the Old Testament Bible. Furthermore, we will explore the concept of spiritual discernment and its profound connection to innovation, creativity, and entrepreneurial thinking. Additionally we will draw inspiration from the prophet Daniel and successful business leaders, to discover the methods of discernment that can guide us in navigating the ever-changing landscapes of life and business.

The Sons of Issachar: Ancestry and Wisdom

The tribe of Issachar was one of the twelve tribes of Israel, tracing their ancestry back to Jacob, the Father of the 12 Tribes of Israel. Let's explore some significant instances where Issachar or their tribe displayed unmatched wisdom and understanding:

a) *Genesis 49:14-15*: 14 "Issachar is a strong donkey, Lying down between two burdens; 15 He saw that rest was good, And that the land was pleasant; He bowed his shoulder to bear a burden, And became a band of slaves.

In Jacob's blessing to his sons, he described Issachar as a strong donkey, resting between the sheepfolds. This imagery signifies their ability to patiently observe and understand the times.

b) **Judges 5:15** And the princes of Issachar were with Deborah; As

Issachar, so was Barak Sent into the valley under his command; Among the divisions of Reuben There were great resolves of heart.

During the time of Deborah and Barak between 1200-1125 B.C.E, the tribe of Issachar joined the battle against their oppressors. Their discernment of the times led them to make strategic decisions that contributed to victory.

Discerning Times and Seasons: Meaning and Significance

1 Chronicles 12:32 speaks of the sons of Issachar who had understanding of the times, to know what Israel ought to do, their chiefs were two hundred; and all their brethren were at their command;

The Sons of Issachar are commended for their understanding of the times to know what Israel should do. Let's delve into the significance of discerning times and seasons:

a) **Knowing Times and Seasons:** Understanding times and seasons involves perceiving the cultural, social, and spiritual context in which one exists. It requires a heightened awareness of the present moment, recognizing both challenges and opportunities. We will explore ways to do this for yourself later in the book.

b) **Spiritual Discernment:** Spiritual discernment goes beyond mere human observation. It is a gift from God, allowing us to perceive the deeper spiritual truths and navigate God's will. It involves seeking wisdom through prayer, studying God's Word, and listening to the promptings of the Holy Spirit. Spiritual Discernment also includes interpreting dreams and visions that may relate to present or future challenges.

Daniel: Discernment and Prosperity

The prophet Daniel, who lived between roughly 620 and 538 B.C.E, exemplified the discernment of times and seasons in his life. His life shifted based upon key moments where Daniel rightly understood the season of a kingdom and took steps for prosperity:

Daniel's Interpretation of Nebuchadnezzar's Dream (Daniel 2):

Daniel 2:1 Now in the second year of Nebuchadnezzar's reign, Nebuchadnezzar had dreams; and his spirit was so troubled that his sleep left him. 2 Then the king gave the command to call the magicians, the astrologers, the sorcerers, and the Chaldeans to tell the king his dreams. So they came and stood before the king. 3 And the king said to them, "I have had a dream, and my spirit is anxious to know the dream." 4 Then the Chaldeans spoke to the king in Aramaic, "O king, live forever! Tell your servants the dream, and we will give the interpretation." 5 The king answered and said to the Chaldeans, "My decision is firm: if you do not make known the dream to me, and its interpretation, you shall be cut in pieces, and your houses shall be made an ash heap. 6 However, if you tell the dream and its interpretation, you shall receive from me gifts, rewards, and great honor. Therefore tell me the dream and its interpretation."

Daniel 2:16 So Daniel went in and asked the king to give him time, that he might tell the king the interpretation. 17 Then Daniel went to his house, and made the decision known to Hananiah, Mishael, and Azariah, his companions, 18 that they might seek mercies from the God of heaven concerning this secret, so that Daniel and his companions might not perish with the rest of the wise men of Babylon. 19 Then the secret was revealed to Daniel in a night vision. So Daniel blessed the God of heaven.

Daniel discerned the meaning of Nebuchadnezzar's dream and correctly interpreted the future rise and fall of kingdoms. His discernment allowed him to offer wise counsel and secure a prominent position in the Babylonian empire.

Daniel's Understanding of the Times (Daniel 9):

Daniel 9: 20 Now while I was speaking, praying, and confessing my sin and the sin of my people Israel, and presenting my supplication before the Lord my God for the holy mountain of my God, 21 yes, while I was speaking in prayer, the man Gabriel, whom I had seen in the vision at the beginning, being caused to fly swiftly, reached me about the time of the evening offering. 22 And he informed me, and talked with me, and said, "O Daniel, I have now come forth to give you skill to understand. 23 At the beginning of your supplications the command went out, and I have come to tell you, for you are greatly beloved; therefore consider the matter, and understand the vision:

Through his study of the Scriptures, prayer and angelic response, Daniel discerned that the seventy-year period of exile prophesied by Jeremiah was coming to an end. He sought God's mercy and guidance, leading to the restoration of Jerusalem.

Methods of Discernment: Biblical Wisdom and Business Acumen

Discerning times and seasons extends beyond spiritual matters. Successful business leaders also possess the ability to interpret financial and economic signs. Let's explore methods of discernment from both biblical wisdom and business wisdom using this tool

Method	Description
Prayer and Meditation	Seek divine guidance through prayer and meditation. Open your heart and mind to receive insights from God.
Study and Reflection	Engage in in-depth study of God's Word and reflect on its timeless wisdom. Allow biblical principles to shape your understanding of the world.

Market Research	Conduct thorough market research to identify trends, consumer preferences, and economic indicators. Stay informed about the changing dynamics of your industry and socio-economic climate.
Networking and Mentoring	Surround yourself with wise and experienced individuals who can offer guidance and share their insights. Seek mentorship from seasoned professionals.
Data Analysis	Utilize data analytics to identify patterns, make informed decisions, and adapt to market conditions. Analyze relevant financial and economic data to identify opportunities and mitigate risks.

Exercise and Reflection

In every season of life, leaders and creatives are called to read both spiritual signals and real-world signs. This tool draws from Chapter 1's key insights on how individuals like the Sons of Issachar and Daniel discerned their times to respond strategically. Use this worksheet to clarify the timing, preparation, and purpose in your current season.

Use the table below to map your current observations, insights, and next steps:

Area of Life / Work	What's Happening? (Trends / Life/ World / Shifts)	Spiritual Insight / Dream / Scripture	What Season Am I In?	Next Strategic Action

Take a look at a few questions that will assist with deeper reflection.

Activation Questions

1. What signs or shifts suggest a change in your current season?
2. Have you received any dreams or scriptures that need revisiting?
3. Which discernment tool do you rely on most—and which is missing?
4. Where are you reacting instead of discerning?
5. Could your current burden point to a calling?
6. What's your next bold prayer for clarity—like Daniel's?
7. Who helps you discern—and who might need your insight?

Chapter Summary

In this chapter, we journeyed through the captivating story of the Sons of Issachar, exploring their ancestral wisdom and discernment. We discovered the profound meaning of discerning times and seasons, drawing insights from biblical accounts and the life of Daniel. Spiritual discernment emerged as a powerful tool for innovation, creativity, and entrepreneurial thinking, guiding us to make wise decisions aligned with God's purposes.

We also explored methods of discernment, combining biblical wisdom with business acumen. Through prayer, study, research, networking, and data analysis, we can develop a well-rounded approach to discerning times and seasons in both spiritual and practical contexts.

As we embrace the legacy of the Sons of Issachar, may we seek divine insight, harness the power of discernment, and navigate the ever-changing landscapes of life and business with confidence and wisdom.

CHAPTER 2:
THE POWER OF
PERCEPTION:

*Training Your Eyes to See
and Make Associations*

"What if your pressure was designed to develop your potential, not destroy your possibilities?"

That question has stayed with me for years. It was the fire that fueled the story of Joseph—an ancient biblical figure known for his rise from slavery and prison to leadership in Egypt. Before he solved national problems, he learned how to see beyond the obvious. He didn't just observe what was happening; he made connections, interpreted patterns, and offered solutions rooted in his relationship with God.

This chapter is about developing that same skill in you—whether you're an entrepreneur, team leader, creative professional, or simply someone navigating the complexities of life and work. We'll draw from both modern psychology and timeless biblical examples.

Perception Begins With Curiosity and Hunger

The journey of seeing differently doesn't start with your eyes—it starts with a mindset. A mindset that is hungry to understand, curious to explore, and willing to look beyond the surface.

The Bible affirms this kind of hunger. Joel 2:28 says, "And afterward, I will pour out My Spirit on all people. Your sons and daughters will prophesy, your old men will dream dreams, your young men will see visions." This was echoed in Acts 2, where Peter explains that divine insight—dreams, visions, prophecy—has been made available to all believers.

Biblically, hunger often precedes revelation. Moses' encounter at the burning bush (Exodus 3), Elijah's still small voice moment (1 Kings 19), and Daniel's insight into end-times prophecy (Daniel 10) all began with intense hunger, prayer, and a desire to understand.

Most people ignore the subtle thoughts, random dreams, or

unexpected connections that come to mind during the day. But those flickers of insight are often the spark of creative breakthrough. Innovation begins when we pause long enough to ask, "What if this moment means more than I realize?"

Developing the Ability to See Differently

Just like physical muscles grow through practice, your mental and spiritual muscles grow through intentional habits. The next two habits help you to do just that.

1. Ask Better Questions

Biblically, Solomon modeled this beautifully. In 1 Kings 3:9, he prayed, "Give your servant a discerning heart to govern your people and to distinguish between right and wrong." He didn't ask for wealth or power—he asked to see clearly.

His request pleased God so much that it unlocked not only discernment but also wealth, peace, and fame. Solomon's story reminds us: vision invites provision.

Breakthrough starts by asking smarter questions:

- What is really going on beneath this challenge?
- What patterns do I keep noticing?
- What is this situation trying to teach me?

Insight: If you're constantly doing without pausing to reflect, you're just reacting—not leading.

2. Write Down What You See and Feel

Habakkuk 2:2 says, "Write the vision and make it plain on tablets, that he may run who reads it." Writing is not just about memory—it's about stewardship. If God can trust you with insight in pieces, He will reveal the whole picture in time.

Consider the faithfulness of the prophets who wrote down dreams and visions that didn't come to pass for decades—or even centuries. Faithfulness to document is a prerequisite for greater clarity.

Insight Trigger	What You Noticed	What It Might Mean	Next Step
Random memory resurfaced	Childhood hobby came to mind	Passion you left behind?	Revisit this activity or skill
Urge to call someone	Persistent thought	Relationship needs attention	Reach out and check in

Randomness Can Be Strategic

One of the most valuable habits of top innovators is something researchers call **Forced Association**—the ability to make meaningful connections between unrelated things.

Biblically, this is demonstrated in Genesis 41, where Joseph interpreted Pharaoh's dream using association:

- Seven fat cows = seven good years
- Seven gaunt cows = seven years of famine

He connected symbolic images to literal meaning, saving an entire region from collapse.

Forced Association also reflects Proverbs 25:2—"It is the glory of God to conceal a matter; to search out a matter is the glory of kings." God often speaks in clues and parables so that those who truly desire understanding will dig for it. Below is an exercise that can be used to cultivate the skill of forced association.

Practice: The 7-Day Forced Association Journal

Sometimes the best ideas are hiding in plain sight—right next to something that seems completely unrelated.

Forced Association is the practice of deliberately pairing your current challenge with a random object, image, or phrase. It's not about being random for randomness' sake—it's about training your mind (and spirit) to see unexpected connections, just like

Joseph interpreting Pharaoh's dream, or Jesus teaching deep truths through everyday items like mustard seeds, coins, or fig trees.

This tool helps you break linear thinking, spark creativity, and hear God through the ordinary.

Day	Current Challenge	Random Source (Book/Magazine)	Random Word/ Object	What Could It Symbolize?	New Insight or Idea
1	Overwhelmed at work	Travel magazine	Compass	Direction, clarity	Revisit my priorities this week
2	Family tension	DIY catalog	Broken shelf	Fragility, overloading	Simplify expectations at home
3	Financial uncertainty	Newspaper headline	Bridge	Transition, connection	Explore partnerships or new income path
4	Creative block	Children's book	Puzzle	Missing piece, playful insight	Try a new medium or ask someone for input
5	Conflict with a friend	Recipe card	Simmer	Slow build-up, emotional heat	Pause and cool off before responding
6	Lack of motivation	Junk mail	Expired coupon	Missed opportunity, timing	Reassess timing—maybe it's not the season
7	Feeling spiritually dry	Gardening catalog	Seed packet	Potential, unseen growth	Trust what's planted, keep watering it

Set a 15-minute timer daily. Flip to a random page. Ask: "God, what could You be showing me through this?"

Emotional Intelligence: Seeing What Others Miss

In 1 Corinthians 12:8–10, Paul describes several spiritual gifts that relate to perception:

- **Word of Knowledge** – Supernatural awareness of a current or past reality
- **Word of Wisdom** – Insight on how to apply knowledge or what to do next

These are not just for church use. They are meant for leadership, business, innovation, counseling, and parenting—anywhere you need strategic insight.

Definitions:

- **Word of Knowledge**: When God supernaturally reveals something you could not know naturally (John 4, Jesus with the Samaritan woman).
- **Word of Wisdom**: When God gives you clarity on how to apply knowledge or what decision to make (Joseph in Genesis 41).

The following table breaks these two spiritual insight gifts down further.

Type of Insight	Description	Biblical Example	Modern Application
Word of Knowledge	Knowing hidden facts	Jesus knowing the Samaritan woman's history (John 4)	Knowing a team member is struggling even if they say they're fine
Word of Wisdom	Knowing what to do	Joseph's food storage plan in Egypt	Creating a budget or solution before crisis hits

Creating the Right Conditions for Insight

You can't expect brilliant ideas to come in chaos. You must train your atmosphere.

The Bible gives examples of dreams and insight occurring in rest:

- Daniel received visions at night (Daniel 7)
- Solomon's famous wisdom request came in a dream (1 Kings 3)
- Jacob's ladder encounter came during sleep (Genesis 28)

Dreams are not an afterthought in Scripture. They are divine tools of communication.

Tips to Trigger Better Thinking:

- **Wind down** with silence, prayer, or calming music
- **Avoid overstimulation** (screens, noise, anxiety triggers)
- **Journal dreams or ideas** as soon as you wake up

Ask yourself:

- What new problems am I facing?
- What have I been avoiding or tolerating?
- What is one idea I've been putting off exploring?

Making Association a Lifestyle

Here's a weekly rhythm you can implement to become a better seer, thinker, and problem-solver:

Weekly Innovation Practice

1. **Pick a challenge** – Big or small (personal or work-related)
2. **Daily Practice** – Open a random page, image, or object
3. **Reflect and Record** – Use the 7-day journal table
4. **Act** – Choose one insight to apply each week

Bonus Tip: Review your entries at the end of the week. Patterns will begin to emerge.

Real-World Example: The Solomon Strategy

In 1 Kings 3:5–13, Solomon is visited by God in a dream. He humbly admits, "I do not know how to go out or come in." In response, God grants him a discerning heart and extraordinary wisdom.

Takeaway: When we ask for discernment, God often gives us more than insight—He gives us influence, provision, and peace. We must have the humility to admit when we don't know, and the hunger to ask God for what we need.

Solomon's request was not selfish. He asked for understanding to serve others. That's the key. When your motive is to benefit others, God often gives you more than you asked.

Expanding Creative Perception: 3 Practices to Train Your Seeing

Before we close this chapter, here are three practical exercises to stretch your creative perception and strengthen how you make associations.

Idea Doodling

Take 10–15 minutes to visually sketch your thoughts or ideas.

Use lines, shapes, and symbols to represent what you're thinking about. Add color or imagery if you like. The goal isn't artistic—it's about expressing ideas that don't fit neatly into words.

Why it works: Doodling activates a different part of your brain. It often helps reveal connections or insights hidden in your subconscious.

Question Storming

Choose a challenge or area where you feel stuck. Instead of brainstorming answers, brainstorm 20–30 open-ended questions. Start with "What if...", "Why not...", or "How might we...?"

Why it works: Questions open the door for new perspectives. They disrupt assumptions and lead to deeper understanding.

The 100 Ideas Challenge

Pick a challenge or opportunity. Write 100 ideas—good, bad, silly, or wild. Don't edit or judge. Just list them. Then go back later and highlight the 3–5 most interesting ideas.

Why it works: Quantity leads to quality. Creative breakthroughs often hide behind your 73rd or 88th idea —not the first five.

Take a look at a few of these questions that will assist with deeper reflection.

Activation Questions

1. What challenge or question are you currently facing?
2. Have you asked God for insight about it directly?
3. What are some "random" thoughts, dreams, or moments that might carry more meaning than you've given them?
4. Can you commit to 15 minutes of creative journaling per day for the next week?
5. Are you honoring the insights God gives by writing them

down and acting on them?

Chapter Summary

- Insight starts with hunger and humility
- Forced Association is a creative and spiritual discipline
- God speaks in patterns—dreams, symbols, and metaphors
- Spiritual insight can lead to strategic advantage in life and leadership

You may not be stuck—you may just need to look at your challenge from a different angle—and from a higher perspective.

Assignment: 7-Day Insight Challenge

Goal: Develop new ideas or solutions for a current challenge.

Steps:

- Choose one area of your life or work to focus on
- Use a random book, article, or object each day
- Ask God what it might symbolize or teach you
- Fill in the 7-Day Journal
- Reflect, connect, and act on at least one insight by the end of the week

In the next chapter, we'll explore how to connect your dreams, pain points, and passions into an innovation blueprint that helps you create with purpose.

Your power to solve problems isn't missing—it's waiting to be trained—and inspired by the same Spirit that led Joseph, Solomon, Daniel, and others to unlock wisdom that changed history.

CHAPTER 3:
AWARENESS:

The Hidden Key to Breakthrough

"Surely the Lord was in this place, and I was not aware of it."
— Jacob (Genesis 28:16)

The Sleep Cycle: Where Awareness Awakens

True awareness isn't just something we develop while awake. In fact, our brains and spirits continue to process insight, emotion, and direction while we sleep. God, in His design, created a rhythm of rest that is deeply connected to our creativity and clarity.

The 4 stages of sleep—especially REM—are not just biological; they're spiritual opportunities. Awareness grows when we understand the cycle behind how dreams arrive. Below is a chart to help you become more aware of what's happening while you sleep:

Sleep Stage	Type	Body & Brain Activity	What It Does	Dreamer Code Parallel
Stage 1 (N1)	Light Sleep (Non-REM)	Muscles relax, heart rate slows	Transitional—initiates sleep	Letting go—stepping into deeper self-awareness
Stage 2 (N2)	Light Sleep (Non-REM)	Brain activity slows with bursts	Supports memory and learning	Early creative downloads begin
Stage 3 (N3)	Deep Sleep (Non-REM)	Physical repair, hormone release	Restores body, deep memory formation	Internal reset—spiritual preparation
Stage 4 (REM)	REM Sleep	Brain highly active, vivid dreams	Emotional healing, creativity, dreaming	Divine insight, prophetic or creative breakthroughs

As you grow in awareness of these stages, you'll begin to recognize when your most vivid and meaningful dreams are likely occurring —and why they feel so powerful. Your dream life isn't an interruption to awareness; it's an invitation to expand it. Every sleep cycle is a potential encounter with divine creativity.

Awareness is the capacity to perceive what's really happening around and within you. It's the ability to slow down, notice patterns, and detect needs, problems, or divine moments before they escalate, disappear, or pass you by.

Types of awareness include:

- **Self-awareness** – recognizing your emotional, mental, and physical state
- **Social awareness** – tuning into others' moods, behaviors, or needs
- **Environmental awareness** – observing what's going on around you

- **Spiritual awareness** – discerning what God is doing or saying in the moment

Sitting at the Door

Years ago, my wife Jojo and I made a tradition out of visiting new restaurants. And without fail, I'd always pick the seat facing the door. She'd laugh about it, but it wasn't random.

I wasn't trying to be dramatic or overprotective. It was about **care**. I wanted to be aware—who was coming in, what was shifting in the room, how we were experiencing the moment together.

That small, instinctive act—sitting in a seat of awareness— reminds me today that so many of our daily decisions hinge on what we *notice*. What we're tuned into. What we allow ourselves to become present to.

That's the key to everything that follows in this chapter.

Why Awareness Is a Spiritual and Strategic Superpower

Proverbs 29:18 says:

> "Where there is no vision, the people perish."
> Another version says: "Where there is no revelation, the people cast off restraint."

Without awareness, we drift.

Without clarity, we self-destruct.

Without attention, we miss God's direction.

Business and Leadership Examples

- **Howard Schultz (Starbucks):** He saw more than coffee. After a trip to Italy, he became aware of the café culture— the atmosphere of warmth, community, and rhythm. Schultz realized that people didn't just want caffeine—they wanted

connection. He brought that awareness home and built Starbucks into a global brand centered around the "third place" between work and home.

- **Sara Blakely (SPANX):** Sara worked selling fax machines and had no fashion background. One day, preparing for a party, she cut the feet off her pantyhose to wear under white pants. That moment of **pain-point awareness** sparked a billion-dollar idea. She saw a problem no one had addressed and turned discomfort into innovation.

- **Oprah Winfrey:** Her unmatched gift wasn't just interviewing—it was **emotional awareness**. She listened deeply and sensed what wasn't being said. Her show became a cultural phenomenon because it gave voice to what others only felt. Awareness made her a trusted presence in millions of lives.

- **Steve Jobs (Apple):** Known for his obsession with simplicity, Jobs constantly asked: "What's getting in the way of experience?" His awareness of user frustration led to revolutionary product design.

In every case, awareness preceded innovation.

Take a look at how awareness was realized in a powerful moment from Jacob's life in the Bible.

Jacob: God Was There All Along

(Historical Timeframe: ~1900 BC)

Jacob was on the run—from family tension, a broken relationship with his brother Esau, and an unclear future. He reached a certain place, took a stone for a pillow, and fell asleep.

Genesis 28:10-11: Now Jacob went out from Beersheba and went toward Haran. So he came to a certain place and stayed there all night, because the sun had set. And he took one of the stones of that place and put it at his head, and he lay down in that place to sleep.

Genesis 28:12: Then he dreamed, and behold, a ladder was set up on the earth, and its top reached to heaven; and there the angels of God were ascending and descending on it.

Genesis 28:13-14: And behold, the Lord stood above it and said: "I am the Lord God of Abraham your father and the God of Isaac; the land on which you lie I will give to you and your descendants. Also your descendants shall be as the dust of the earth; you shall spread abroad to the west and the east, to the north and the south; and in you and in your seed all the families of the earth shall be blessed.

Genesis 28:15: Behold, I am with you and will keep you wherever you go, and will bring you back to this land; for I will not leave you until I have done what I have spoken to you."

Genesis 28:16-17: Then Jacob awoke from his sleep and said, "Surely the Lord is in this place, and I did not know it." And he was afraid and said, "How awesome is this place! This is none other than the house of God, and this is the gate of heaven!"

Jacob's lack of awareness almost cost him a sacred moment. He didn't feel divine. He didn't sense it ahead of time. It was only *after* that he realized what he was in the middle of.

Jacob's story teaches us:

- You can be in the middle of divine activity and not know it.
- God often reveals Himself *after* you've quieted down.
- Your current discomfort could be holy ground.

Jacob marked the place with a stone pillar and made a vow: If God would guide and provide, he would serve Him. His awareness became the foundation for transformation. His awareness became the foundation for transformation.

Nehemiah: Awareness That Leads to Strategy

(Historical Timeframe: ~445 BC)

Nehemiah was serving as a cupbearer in Persia—an

administrative role of trust and proximity to power. When his brother returned from Jerusalem and reported that the city walls were broken and its people vulnerable, Nehemiah didn't respond with logic or detachment.

Nehemiah 1:1-3: The words of Nehemiah the son of Hachaliah. It came to pass in the month of Chislev, in the twentieth year, as I was in Shushan the citadel, that Hanani one of my brethren came with men from Judah; and I asked them concerning the Jews who had escaped, who had survived the captivity, and concerning Jerusalem. And they said to me, "The survivors who are left from the captivity in the province are there in great distress and reproach. The wall of Jerusalem is also broken down, and its gates are burned with fire."

Nehemiah 1:4: So it was, when I heard these words, that I sat down and wept, and mourned for many days; I was fasting and praying before the God of heaven.

Awareness led to intercession. Intercession led to strategy.

Nehemiah 2:1-3: And it came to pass in the month of Nisan, in the twentieth year of King Artaxerxes, when wine was before him, that I took the wine and gave it to the king. Now I had never been sad in his presence before. Therefore the king said to me, "Why is your face sad, since you are not sick? This is nothing but sorrow of heart." So I became dreadfully afraid, and said to the king, "May the king live forever! Why should my face not be sad, when the city, the place of my fathers' tombs, lies waste, and its gates are burned with fire?"

Nehemiah 2:4-5: Then the king said to me, "What do you request?" So I prayed to the God of heaven. And I said to the king, "If it pleases the king, and if your servant has found favor in your sight, I ask that you send me to Judah, to the city of my fathers' tombs, that I may rebuild it."

Nehemiah 4:17: Those who built on the wall, and those who

carried burdens, loaded themselves so that with one hand they worked at construction, and with the other held a weapon.

Nehemiah returned, assessed the damage firsthand, and motivated the people to rise and work.

But resistance came. Enemies mocked. Workers grew tired. Fear crept in.

So Nehemiah adapted. Half the people built while the other half held weapons. He made space for both *progress* and *protection*.

Key Awareness Lessons from Nehemiah:

- He paid attention to what others overlooked.
- He felt deeply but acted wisely.
- He didn't spiritualize away the problem—he mobilized a solution.
- He stayed alert when opposition came.

Before diving into the tools of awareness, it's important to understand that these exercises aren't just random tasks—they're strategic steps in training your perception. Let's begin with a visual framework to help you process what awareness looks like in motion.

The Awareness Pyramid

This pyramid represents how awareness builds from the ground up. At the base is your attention to what's broken or overlooked—where transformation often begins. At the top is your ability to act and protect what matters.

Pyramid Top – BUILD AND GUARD
Act on what you notice and protect what's sacred

OBSERVE OTHERS ACTIVELY
Watch behaviors, tone, fatigue, and unspoken needs

SEE OBSTACLES AS OPPORTUNITIES

Shift your mindset: "What can I learn here?"

PAY ATTENTION TO WHAT'S NOT WORKING
Identify repeated breakdowns or tension points

Pyramid Base – CHASE THE ANOMALY
Investigate what feels off—pain points often point to divine insight

Four Awareness Practices You Can Build Now
The next four practices will help you implement awareness on a daily basis. These questions and habits are meant to spark realignment, reflection, and practical growth.

1. Chase the Anomaly

God often highlights what's *off* as a doorway to discover His wisdom.

Ask:

- What feels misaligned?
- What keeps getting ignored?
- What's not "adding up"?

2. Pay Attention to What's Not Working

Nehemiah noticed broken systems and tired people.

Ask:

- What's draining my energy every week?
- What system in my life keeps producing frustration?
- Am I tolerating dysfunction because I fear change?

3. See Obstacles as Opportunities

Obstacle Language:

- "This always happens to me."
- "I'll never get ahead."

Opportunity Language:

- "What's the growth lesson in this?"
- "How might I pivot?"

4. Observe Others Actively

Jesus noticed people others overlooked. You can do the same.

Ask:

- What are people NOT saying?
- What behavior is masking burnout or fear?
- What do people consistently turn to me for?

Before you move into the next tools, it's critical to name what blocks awareness. These three common barriers often shut down insight before it begins.

Barriers to Awareness

1. **Assumptions** – Jumping to conclusions without full context
2. **Defensiveness** – Reacting to correction instead of processing it
3. **Ego** – Thinking you already know everything God or others might say

Ask: *Is my inner noise louder than God's whisper?*

Let's take these insights into real-world strategy. These scenarios show how awareness functions in everyday entrepreneurship, team leadership, and innovation.

Expanded Business Applications

- Great entrepreneurs **study what people complain about**
- Great marketers **track anomalies in user behavior**
- Great team leaders **notice when morale shifts subtly**

One powerful yet often overlooked source of innovation is the diversity within a team. Studies show that teams made up of individuals from different ethnic, generational, and socio-economic backgrounds are more likely to develop creative, market-relevant solutions. For example, a group of friends in a multiethnic neighborhood of Atlanta noticed a disconnect between youth and the tech job market. By combining their unique experiences—one was a teacher, one worked in IT, one had a background in ministry—they co-launched a community coding bootcamp that now feeds talent directly into local startups. Their innovation didn't come from similarity; it came from the synergy of diverse perspectives.

In your own setting, this might look like convening three people with completely different life experiences—maybe a retiree, a high school student, and a small business owner—to help you reimagine how your church or organization engages the community. You don't need a grant to do that. Just the humility to listen and the courage to act.

You can even use simple frameworks like **triad teams**—groups of three with intentionally varied perspectives—or **cross-generational pods** where a teen, an adult, and an elder reflect on the same issue. These models have been used in both churches and startups to surface fresh insight and increase buy-in from the people they're serving.

Your **profit**, **peace**, or **purpose** might be one layer of awareness away.

Exercises and Reflections
This table allows you to reflect in real time on the events that shape your week. Use it to practice self-evaluation, pattern recognition, and growth tracking.

Self-Awareness Journal Table

Situation	What Happened	What I Noticed	What I Felt	How I Responded	What I'll Change

To deepen your awareness muscle, here's a challenge you can do this week. Focus on what you often overlook, and give it your full attention. One moment each day could reveal a breakthrough.

7-Day Awareness Challenge

Each day, reflect on just one interaction, environment, or moment you often overlook.

Day	Moment	What I Noticed Differently	Action or Prayer
1			
2			
3			
4			
5			
6			
7			

Activation Questions

1. What has God or life been trying to show you repeatedly?
2. Where are you emotionally numb or mentally distracted?
3. What person or project have you assumed you fully understand—but maybe haven't explored deeply?
4. How can you shift from obstacle language to opportunity language?
5. What "door-facing" decision—like my restaurant habit—do you need to make in your life right now?

Prayer

"God, help me to slow down and become aware—not just of what's broken, but of what You're building. Open my eyes to what You're doing in me and around me."

Chapter Summary

- Awareness is where innovation, strategy, and discernment begin
- Jacob and Nehemiah show how awareness leads to divine encounters and public breakthroughs

- Business & faith leaders thrive on intentional perception
- Tools like the Awareness Pyramid help make this process clear and repeatable
- Awareness doesn't just change your thoughts—it changes your life

CHAPTER 4: MAPPING DREAMS, PAIN POINTS & PASSIONS

"Then Joseph said to Pharaoh, 'The dreams of Pharaoh are one; God has shown Pharaoh what He is about to do.'"
— Genesis 41:25 (NKJV)

A Dream That Changed Everything

I never expected a dream to change the course of my life—but it did. In late 2014, I had several dreams over time that felt too specific to ignore. They weren't just abstract symbols or emotional echoes of the day. These dreams were vivid. I saw **specific people**. I viewed **specific places in Southeast Wisconsin**. I experienced the pain of lives being lost without the hope of Jesus. I felt a **passion for multiethnic unity** rise inside me that hadn't yet found expression in my daily life.

The dreams spilled over into my daily life. I could not focus at my day job. I was showing up in the parking lot in tears with a burning heart to see people from diverse backgrounds experience the love of God. These dreams led me to **pay attention**, to **listen**, and to **act in faith**. That journey became the origin of City of Light Church —a faith community planted in the heart of one of the most segregated regions in the United States, built on the conviction that what God reveals in dreams can become a roadmap for real-world change.

Why Dreams, Pain Points & Passions Matter

Dreams, pain points, and passions are **not random**. They are often **God's way of surfacing clues** to your calling.

- **Dreams** give insight about what God is revealing (Genesis 37, Joel 2, Acts 2)
- **Pain points** show where the world is groaning for solutions (Romans 8:22)
- **Passions** uncover what energizes you for long-term impact (Psalm 37:4)

The intersection of these three is where innovation, purpose, and clarity begin to form.Let's look at how the Bible models this process—and how you can apply it.

Joseph's Blueprint for Mapping Dreams

Genesis 37:5–11 (NKJV)

> "Now Joseph had a dream, and he told it to his brothers; and they hated him even more. So he said to them, 'Please hear this dream which I have dreamed: There we were, binding sheaves in the field. Then behold, my sheaf arose and also stood upright; and indeed your sheaves stood all around and bowed down to my sheaf.'"

Joseph saw **a symbolic image**: stalks of grain bowing down. Later, he saw **stars and the sun and moon** bowing to his own.

Key insight? He didn't yet **understand** what it meant, but he **recorded and shared it**. Years later, these images made sense.

Joseph teaches us:

1. Write the dream down.
2. Ask God for clarity—but don't force it.
3. Let life unfold. Meaning will emerge over time.

Dreams in Scripture: More Than Symbols

God frequently uses dreams as **communication tools** in critical moments:

- **Jacob's Ladder** – Genesis 28
- **Joseph the Carpenter** – Matthew 1–2 (Dreams warned and directed him to protect Jesus)
- **Nebuchadnezzar's Dream** – Daniel 2
- **Paul's Macedonian Call** – Acts 16

Dreams are:

- Timely
- Spirit-led
- Directional

They are not just "imagination." They can be **invitations to partner with Heaven**.

The Dream Mapping Process

Dreams aren't just symbolic—they're **strategic**. Whether you're spiritual or skeptical, dreams often surface emotional, spiritual, or creative data your conscious mind misses. Mapping them can uncover patterns and next steps.

Here's a simple framework:

Dream Detail	Possible Symbolism	Current Emotion	Associated Person/Place	Possible Action
I was walking through an abandoned school	Missed opportunity? Unfinished purpose?	Frustrated, unsettled	My hometown	Revisit a childhood goal or call a mentor
Saw fire consuming a city, but one building stood untouched	Judgment, crisis, protection	Anxiety + hope	My church	Pray for protection and clarity of assignment

Use this table weekly. Even "weird" dreams can become clues over time.

Identifying Pain Points: The Pressure That Pushes Purpose

Joseph's elevation didn't come *because* of his dreams—it came through **interpreting the pain points of others**.

- In prison, he noticed the sadness of two men (Genesis 40)
- He asked questions, listened, and interpreted their dreams
- Later, Pharaoh's confusion became his opportunity

Pain is often the **pressure that pushes purpose forward**.

Ask:

- What frustrates you repeatedly?
- What problems do people constantly bring to you?
- What injustice makes your blood boil?
- What's the *one problem* you'd love to solve, even if no one paid you?

Pain is often the prophetic signal that something must be created or reformed.

Passion: The Fuel That Sustains Innovation

You'll never build anything meaningful long-term without passion. Passion sustains purpose through trial.

Joseph's passion? He loved **bringing order to chaos**.

- In Potiphar's house: He brought order to operations
- In prison: He became trusted by the warden
- In Pharaoh's palace: He created a national food system

He didn't just interpret dreams. He built systems. Here some passion reflection questions:

Ask yourself:

- What do I do that gives me energy—even after a long day?
- What do others always thank me for?
- What themes keep coming up in my conversations and journals?

The Intersection: Where Innovation Lives

The sweet spot is where your:

- **Dreams** (what you're seeing),
- **Pain points** (what breaks your heart), and
- **Passions** (what energizes you)

converge.

Innovation Triangle Diagram:

```
             [DREAMS]

                 ▲
               / \
              /   \
             /     \
[PASSIONS] ------- [PAIN POINTS]
```

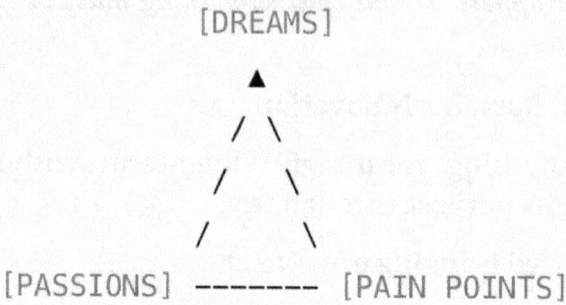

In the middle lies:

"What God might be inviting you to solve or build."

God often communicates to us in symbols. We often see how Jesus used parables and metaphor to draw seekers into a deeper understanding of the mysteries of God. Our dreams/visions are no different. Take a look at some common dream symbols below.

Chart: Common Dream Symbols

Symbol	Possible Biblical Meaning	Application
Water	Spirit, life, cleansing (John 7:38)	Renewal, transition, baptism
Fire	God's presence or judgment (Exodus 3:2)	Purification, urgency
Keys	Authority, access (Isaiah 22:22)	New opportunity, leadership
Storm	Chaos, testing (Mark 4:37–41)	Fear, spiritual warfare
Baby	New beginning, calling (Isaiah 9:6)	New responsibility, ministry

These are not formulas. Pray, ask questions, and consider your personal context.

Exercises

Use a table like this to record your dreams/visions to help you interpret deeper meaning, while recording current pain and passion points of your life:

1. Dream Reflection Table

Dream Snippet	Emotion	Symbol	Who Was There?	What Might It Mean?

2. Pain Point Audit

Write 3 areas where you feel ongoing frustration or compassion.

1.
2.
3.

Now ask: What small, simple action could I take toward a solution?

3. Passion Clues List

- What do you talk about when no one's prompting you?
- What do you do well that others struggle with?
- If money weren't a factor, what would you build or teach?

Activation Questions

1. What dreams have stayed with you over time?
2. What unresolved problems (in your life or others') keep resurfacing?
3. What role might your pain or passion play in God's

purpose for you?

4. Have you invited anyone else to help interpret your dreams or direction?

5. What's one bold step you can take this week to explore your purpose?

Prayer

"God, You speak in visions, symbols, and longings. Help me recognize when You're pointing me toward my purpose—through dreams, pain, and passion. Give me boldness to act, wisdom to wait, and insight to discern what You are doing through my life."

Chapter Summary

- Dreams are one of God's primary tools for direction
- Joseph's life teaches us how to steward dream-data into action
- Pain points reveal purpose areas waiting for innovation
- Passion sustains calling through adversity
- Your story, gifting, and assignment often sit at the intersection of dreams, passion, and pain

In Chapter 5, we'll explore how dreams become strategic tools during times of crisis—and how God still speaks to provide solutions when the world is in famine or fear.

CHAPTER 5: INTERPRETING DREAMS IN TIMES OF CRISIS

"It is not in me; God will give Pharaoh an answer of peace."
— Genesis 41:16 (NKJV)

When the World Is Shaking

During a particularly demanding season of ministry and work, I began to sense a recurring theme in my dreams—only this time, they didn't point to launching something new, but to preserving what was already in motion. One night, I dreamt of a large crowd gathering in a familiar space, only for a sudden storm to scatter them. I woke up with a deep sense that I was being warned—not to panic—but to prepare. That dream set me on a path of proactive leadership—strategizing how to build resilience into our systems, team dynamics, and even my own spiritual rhythms. What I saw in my sleep became a blueprint for stewarding what God had already started.

That's what dreams can do—especially in times of crisis.

Crisis Dreams: When Heaven Interrupts Earth

Throughout the Bible, dreams often show up *right before* major crisis or change.

- **Joseph** interprets Pharaoh's dream of famine and proposes a plan to feed a nation.
- **Daniel** interprets Nebuchadnezzar's dream of empires rising and falling.
- **Joseph the Carpenter** receives divine warning dreams to protect Jesus.
- **Paul** dreams of a Macedonian call that changes the direction of his mission.

These weren't just mystical moments—they were strategic, **heaven-initiated interruptions** in critical times.

> *Dreams in crisis are not to frighten us. They are blueprints for foresight, stewardship, and leadership.*

Joseph's Crisis-Response Model

Pharaoh is terrified by two dreams. His magicians fail. Joseph, still a prisoner, is summoned.

Genesis 41:15–16 (NKJV)

> "Pharaoh said to Joseph, 'I have had a dream, and there is no one who can interpret it. But I have heard it said of you that you can understand a dream, to interpret it.'
> So Joseph answered Pharaoh, saying, 'It is not in me; God will give Pharaoh an answer of peace.'"

Joseph interprets:

- **Seven fat cows / healthy grain** = 7 years of plenty
- **Seven thin cows / withered grain** = 7 years of famine

But interpretation isn't where he stops. He becomes a **crisis planner**:

- Designate overseers
- Collect 20% of harvest during surplus
- Create storehouses
- Prepare for famine before it comes

His discernment saved millions—and promoted him to governor.

From Revelation to Administration

Joseph didn't just reveal the meaning of the dream. He **designed a national economic system** from it.

That's what mature spiritual insight looks like. It doesn't stop with mystery—it builds systems for people to thrive.

This is our invitation too.

Discerning Crisis Dreams in Today's World

You may not be Pharaoh, but if you're a parent, pastor, entrepreneur, teacher, or leader—you're facing complexity and uncertainty.

Some dreams carry weight. They call us to intercede, prepare, pivot, or warn others.

Here's how to recognize a crisis dream:

Signal	Possible Interpretation
Intense emotion upon waking	Urgency for action or prayer
Recurring disaster theme	Pattern, spiritual warfare, systems breaking down
Familiar people in danger	You may be called to intercede
You leading others in chaos	A leadership assignment
Elements of storage or gathering	Preparation for scarcity or change

Not all dreams are warnings—but some are road signs.

The tool below will help interpret intense or disruptive dreams during times of crisis. Each "D" reveals a layer of meaning—from recognizing what's breaking down (Disruption) to discovering God's guidance (Direction). Use it to gain clarity, peace, and a path forward when dreams feel heavy or urgent.

A Crisis Dream Framework: 6 D's

1. **Document**
   Record the dream immediately: who, what, symbols, feelings, setting.
2. **Discern**
   Ask God for clarity. Is this dream for me, someone else, or my community?
3. **Decode**
   Cross-reference symbols with Scripture. Use spiritual mentors if needed.
4. **Discuss**
   Bring it into a trusted community. Discernment often

happens in dialogue.

5. **Design**
   Ask: What response does this dream require? How should I act?

6. **Do**
   Take the first step. Action often brings confirmation.

When the World Is in Famine—Lead

The result of Joseph's preparation was this: Egypt not only survived—but became a *source of provision* for others.

In times of crisis, God often promotes people who can:

- See clearly
- Strategize practically
- Act courageously

God may be speaking to you now in dreams, not only to reveal what's coming—but to **position you to lead**.

Modern Examples: Crisis-Inspired Innovation

1. **Business Leader's Vision**
   A restaurant owner had a recurring dream of feeding lines of people in a storm. It drove him to start a nonprofit kitchen that served thousands during COVID.

2. **Teacher's Dream During Lockdown**
   A woman dreamt of isolated students sitting in darkness. She launched a free tutoring program online. It exploded in reach—because she moved when others froze.

3. **Family Dream of Land**
   A couple repeatedly dreamt of open fields and provision. They left the city, bought rural land, and now run a sustainable farm that supports multiple families.

Don't just write your dream down—**walk it out**.

Exercises & Journaling Tools
Below are several exercises you can use to move from dreams/

vision to actionable steps to help you in your everyday life.

1. Crisis Dream Interpretation Table

This table gives you a structured way to process emotionally intense dreams. By identifying the feeling, theme, symbol, and possible message, you can move from confusion to clarity—and discern how God may be speaking in the middle of crisis.

Dream Scene	Emotional Tone	Possible Symbols	Next Step

2. Crisis Readiness Reflection

This reflection helps you evaluate how mentally, spiritually, and practically prepared you are for unexpected challenges. It invites honest assessment and offers a proactive way to strengthen weak points before a crisis hits—so you're not just reacting, but responding with clarity and faith.

Area of Life	Current Weakness	How Might I Prepare?
Finances	No savings	Start $20/week fund
Community	Lack of support	Reach out to mentor
Faith	Inconsistent	Set prayer rhythm

3. Dream-to-Design Blueprint

These questions help you move from insight to implementation. By connecting what you've seen in your dreams, sensed in your spirit, or wrestled with in your struggles, this blueprint offers a step-by-step map to turn revelation into real-world innovation—whether it's a business, ministry, creative project, or life decision. It's where spiritual clarity meets strategic design.

- What is the most urgent message God has shown you recently?
- What do you need to build in response—spiritually or practically?

- Who can you involve in executing this plan?

Activation Questions

1. Have you had dreams that felt heavier than usual—like warnings?
2. What's a current "famine" in your life or field?
3. Are you waiting for conditions to improve instead of building during scarcity?
4. What would it look like to prepare like Joseph?
5. Who might benefit if you shared your dream?

Prayer

"God, speak to me in crisis the way You did with Joseph. Help me not only hear You, but obey. Give me strategy, courage, and clarity. Let what You show me in the night become what I build in the day. Amen."

Chapter Summary

- God speaks through dreams, especially during crisis
- Joseph models revelation + response → leadership
- Crisis dreams aren't for fear—they're for preparation
- Your dream may be a deliverance plan for others
- Innovation often begins with an interruption

In Chapter 6, we'll explore how **asking better questions** leads to deeper creativity, problem-solving, and breakthrough ideas that don't come from the obvious.

CHAPTER 6: UNLOCKING INNOVATION THROUGH QUESTIONS

"The quality of your questions determines the quality of your solutions." — Tony Robbins

The Questions That Changed Everything

Some of the most important shifts in my life and leadership didn't come from answers—but from hard questions.

One of the biggest was: *"Why is Southeast Wisconsin so siloed— split between the inner city and the suburbs, between historically marginalized communities and those with greater access to resources?"*

That one question sent me down a path of uncovering the history of racially restrictive housing covenants, redlining, and decades of disinvestment that had quietly shaped our region's relational and economic divides. It wasn't just history—it was affecting who interacted, who worshiped together, and who even shopped in the same places.

Instead of staying stuck in frustration, I kept asking, *"Where could we start something different?"* That led to identifying shared spaces where people from both city and suburb felt comfortable: skating rinks, pools, restaurants, and neutral gathering places. From there, we began hosting inclusive, family-friendly events —ice skating nights, pool parties, and game nights—not just as outreach, but as *reconciliation environments*.

Our very first community pool party—*before we had even launched a single Sunday service*—drew nearly **1,000 people**. That moment confirmed what the questions had been pointing to all along: people were hungry for unity, belonging, and safe places to connect across lines of division.

City of Light Church was born in that space between the question and the answer. It's still growing there today.

These kinds of transformational questions are more common than you might think. Let's explore some names of modern innovators with whom you may be familiar:

Everyday Questions That Led to Global Solutions

- **James Dyson** asked, *"Why do vacuum cleaners lose suction?"*

That one question led to 5,127 failed prototypes—and one of the most successful product designs in history.

- **A group of Detroit teens** asked, *"What if we cleaned sneakers instead of waiting for jobs?"* Their shoe restoration business launched from a school locker and now ships nationally.

- **Two broke roommates in San Francisco** asked, *"What if we charged people to sleep on air mattresses?"* That was the seed of **Airbnb**, now valued at over $100 billion.

- **An exhausted mom** asked, *"Why am I always taking care of everyone but myself?"* That journal entry became a coaching business for mothers, started with nothing more than a Canva logo and a YouTube-built website.

Innovation isn't about being smarter than others.
It's about being bold enough to ask better questions.

Why Questions Unlock Innovation

"Why" questions do 4 major things in the lives of those who dare to ask them.

Why Questions:

- Reveal assumptions
- Invite curiosity
- Create space for input
- Spark new solutions

Most people stop questioning when something becomes *functional*. But functionality isn't the same as **thriving**.

The Breakthrough Question Ladder

To go deeper, you must climb higher.

Here's a tool to push your thinking and lead yourself—or your team—into new territory:

Breakthrough Question Ladder

Level	Question Type	Example
1	Clarifying	What am I really trying to solve?
2	Contextual	Who is this affecting most?
3	Challenging Assumptions	What am I assuming that might not be true?
4	Possibility-Oriented	What else could this be?
5	Future-Creating	What would a breakthrough look like?

This ladder is not just for business plans—it's for marriages, ministries, and mindsets.

When you ask higher-level questions, you uncover **hidden constraints** and **unseen solutions**.

Jesus: Master of Strategic Questions

Jesus asked over 300 questions in the gospels. He wasn't looking for information. He was **transforming minds**.

Examples:

- *"Who do you say that I am?"* (Matthew 16:15)
- *"Do you want to be made well?"* (John 5:6)
- *"What do you want Me to do for you?"* (Mark 10:51)

The blind man Bartimaeus shouted for mercy. Jesus asked, *"What do you want?"* Why?

Because clarity is the seedbed for miracles.

> *Questions in the hands of Jesus weren't obstacles. They were doorways to destiny.*

Solomon, known to be the wisest man to ever live, also used

the right questions to transform the world in which he lived.

Solomon's Request: When Solomon could
have asked for anything, he asked:

1 Kings 3:9 (NKJV)

> *"Therefore give to Your servant an understanding heart to judge Your people, that I may discern between good and evil."*

God gave him more than wisdom—He gave him wealth, peace, and legacy.
Why? Because the right question leads to the right reward.

The Reframing Map is designed to help you shift how you interpret challenging or confusing experiences. By walking through this tool, you'll move from seeing problems as roadblocks to recognizing them as redirection points or hidden invitations. It trains your mindset to look at hardship through a lens of purpose, preparation, and potential.

Reflection Tool: The Reframing Map

Here's a practice to shift default thinking:

Problem Statement	New Question	Reframed Opportunity
People don't show up to events	Why would I show up if I were them?	Build events around their actual needs
I keep hitting a money wall	What am I refusing to let go of?	Reimagine my pricing, platform, or partners

Innovation Exercises & Journaling Tools

This section equips you with practical ways to turn ideas into action. Innovation isn't just about big breakthroughs—it starts with simple, consistent habits of writing, reflecting, and stretching your thinking. These tools are meant to help you break creative blockages, generate fresh ideas, and build a rhythm of insight-driven experimentation in your everyday life, business, or leadership.

Question Storming

Unlike traditional brainstorming that focuses on solutions, question storming challenges you to generate as many insightful questions as possible. It trains your brain to explore possibilities, uncover assumptions, and reframe challenges creatively. This tool is powerful for individuals, teams, and dreamers trying to get unstuck or discover new angles.

Choose a challenge you're facing. Instead of brainstorming *answers*, brainstorm *questions*.

Set a 10-minute timer and generate at least 25 open-ended questions. Use starters like:

- What if...
- Why not...
- How might we...

   Why this works: New questions create new pathways in your brain—and spirit.

Reframing Practice

Reframing trains your mind to pivot from discouragement to discovery, from pain to purpose. Instead of asking "Why did this happen to me?" you explore what new meaning, growth, or opportunity may be hidden inside the experience. Try this weekly exercise with your journal or team:

Reframing Examples:

What's Not Working	Default Reaction	New Framing Question	Inspired Action
Low attendance at events	"No one is interested anymore."	"What unmet need could we be overlooking?"	Survey attendees, adjust format to meet real needs.
Team conflict at work	"They just don't get along."	"What strengths are hidden in the tension?"	Host a team insight session to clarify roles.

Slow business growth	"We're failing compared to others."	"What's working well that we can build on?"	Double down on the best-performing product.
Personal burnout	"I'm just not strong enough for this."	"What support or rhythm have I been neglecting?"	Block weekly margin for rest and soul care.

Weekly Question Ladder Practice

Pick one area of your life (home, work, leadership). Climb the question ladder to uncover fresh insight. **Write your answers or voice record them if you process better verbally.**

Activation Questions

1. What big questions are you avoiding because they seem overwhelming?
2. What "why" or "what if" question has been surfacing lately in your spirit?
3. Are you asking low-level questions (How do I get by?) or high-level ones (What would thriving look like?)
4. When Jesus asked, *"What do you want Me to do for you?"*— what's your honest answer?

Prayer

"God, give me the courage to ask better questions. Show me the things I've been afraid to see. Teach me how to uncover Your wisdom through curiosity. And help me lead others not with answers alone—but with insight that creates space for change."

Chapter Summary

- Innovation starts with curiosity—not expertise
- Business breakthroughs, ministries, and movements often begin with one bold question
- Jesus and Solomon both demonstrated the power of intentional inquiry
- Tools like the Breakthrough Question Ladder and Reframing

Map help unlock new vision
- When we ask God *and ourselves* better questions, we open the door to destiny

In Chapter 7, we'll explore how to break mental limits—moving from stuck patterns and "default settings" into discovery, renewal, and reimagined possibilities.

CHAPTER 7: BREAKING MENTAL LIMITS – FROM DEFAULT TO DISCOVERY

"Do not be conformed to this world, but be transformed by the renewing of your mind..."
— Romans 12:2 (NKJV)

Innovation Is Often Stuck Behind Assumptions

Sometimes the thing holding us back isn't a lack of opportunity—it's a story we keep telling ourselves.

Consider these important moments in history:

- **Howard Schultz** didn't just create coffee shops. He broke a mental limit: *"People won't pay $4 for coffee."* He believed people wanted connection and consistency, not just caffeine. The result? Starbucks changed the way the world thinks about morning routines.

- **The Wright Brothers** weren't engineers. They ran a bicycle shop. Everyone else assumed only government-funded experts could build flying machines. They challenged the default belief: *"Humans can't fly."*

- In **New York City**, an organization called **The Knowledge House** was launched to help underserved communities access careers in tech. The founders heard people saying, *"Tech isn't for people like us."* Instead of accepting that narrative, they created free bootcamps, partnered with major tech companies, and equipped youth with the skills to change their own trajectories. Now their alumni are working at places like Google and Amazon.

From Hidden Story to Superpower

I didn't always recognize the strength in my story. I grew up on the rougher side of town, surrounded by poverty, uncertainty, and pressure most kids my age didn't have to carry. For a long time, I thought success meant hiding where I came from—like my past was something I needed to erase in order to move forward.

But the more I reflected, the more I realized: **what I survived became my superpower**.

I had learned to adapt. I had grit. I knew how to grind when others froze—and how to trust God when everything else was shaking. From being the first in my family to graduate college, to stepping into corporate spaces, to leading community efforts that bring hope to families—I began to see that my journey through adversity wasn't a setback. It was preparation.

Maybe you've been afraid of your story. Maybe you've tried to bury the things you've been through, convinced they disqualify you. But what if your struggle is the exact thing God wants to use to strengthen others—and to unlock the leader in you?

Now, I no longer run from my background—I build from it. The real breakthrough came when I challenged the assumption that I had to be someone else to lead effectively. Turns out, the pressure made the leader.

Breaking the Default: What Else Could This Be?

We don't just live in neighborhoods. We live in **narratives**.

- *"I'm not good with money."*
- *"I'm not a creative person."*
- *"People like me don't get ahead."*

These aren't just thoughts. They're agreements. And they become mental ceilings. But what if your ceiling was actually the floor for something new?

Here are a few tools to help break through:

Reframing Tool: "What Else Could This Be?"
This tool helps you slow down your assumptions and open your mind to new interpretations when you're facing tension, confusion, or conflict. Instead of reacting based on your default mindset, you ask:

"What else could this be besides what I first assumed?"

Default Assumption	What Else Could It Be?	New Possibility
"They didn't text back—must be mad."	"Maybe they're overwhelmed."	Opportunity to show grace
"I failed at this last year."	"Maybe that version wasn't the right fit."	Try again with new insight
"No one showed up to the event."	"Maybe we picked the wrong format."	Rethink location, partners, timing

This tool invites humility, grace, and courage—all of which fuel innovation.

The Assumption Flip

This is a rapid reframing technique used to challenge the "default beliefs" you carry into situations—especially under pressure. Often, the biggest block to breakthrough isn't the problem itself, but the story you've told yourself about it.

Take one of your strongest limiting beliefs:

Ask:
"What if the opposite were true?"

Limiting Belief	Flip It	What Changes?
"I'm not a leader."	"I influence people every day."	You start owning your voice
"I don't have enough money."	"I have enough to start something small."	You start with what you have
"They won't listen to me."	"I haven't told the right story yet."	You reframe your pitch or vision

This isn't delusion—it's **mental creativity with spiritual authority**.

The Bible's Pattern of Limit Breaking

Scripture is filled with people who believed the wrong thing—

until God showed them otherwise.

Gideon: "I'm the Least"

Judges 6:15 (NKJV)

> "So he said to Him, 'O my Lord, how can I save Israel? Indeed my clan is the weakest in Manasseh, and I am the least in my father's house.'"

Gideon was hiding in fear, threshing wheat in a winepress. But God called him *a mighty warrior*—not based on performance, but on purpose.

God didn't change Gideon's environment. He changed his identity first.

Peter: "I'm Too Broken"

Peter denied Jesus three times. But after the resurrection, Jesus meets him again—not with condemnation, but with **questions**.

> *"Do you love Me?"* (John 21:15–17)

Peter's failure didn't define him—his response to restoration did. He went on to lead the early church.

The Woman with the Issue of Blood: "I Don't Belong"

She wasn't supposed to be in public. She had no platform, no resources. But she said to herself:

Mark 5:28 (NKJV)

> "If only I may touch His clothes, I shall be made well."

Her miracle didn't begin with a pastor. It began with her inner narrative.

Modern Example: Rewriting the Story in Milwaukee

In Milwaukee, **Arty's Sweet Talk Cupcakes**, owned by Artezia May, is one of many businesses supported by the **Wisconsin Women's Business Initiative Corporation (WWBIC)**. Artezia turned her passion for baking into a thriving business with WWBIC's help through training and financial support. Her story is not just about desserts—it's about defeating discouragement and building a legacy for her family through entrepreneurship.

She once thought, *"Who's really going to take me seriously?"* But with faith, skill, and community backing, she proved that your passion, when nurtured, can rewrite your future.

Reflection Exercise: Default to Discovery

This exercise helps you shift from reactive thinking ("default mode") to curious, intentional thinking ("discovery mode"). Many people respond to difficulty, delay, or disappointment with automatic reactions—defensiveness, discouragement, or self-doubt.

Instead, what if you saw every moment—even the hard ones—as a clue or invitation to discover something new?

This reflection prompts you to identify where you've been on autopilot and replace it with a growth-minded response rooted in learning, faith, and possibility.

Area of Life	Default Belief	Discovery-Based Reframe	New Possibility
Career	"I'm stuck in this job."	"I've learned what I don't want."	Explore a pivot using strengths
Faith	"I'm not spiritual enough."	"God meets me where I am."	Reignite personal prayer life
Finances	"I can't save money."	"I can track $10/week."	Build emergency fund slowly

Weekly Rewiring Challenge

For 7 days, track one limiting thought per day and write a flipped version beneath it.

Day	Limiting Thought	Flip It	Action Step
1	I'm always late.	I'm learning to value time better.	Set alarms 15 mins earlier
2	No one takes me seriously.	I can communicate with clarity.	Practice pitch with a friend
3	I'm not creative.	I'm growing in creative confidence.	Try a 10-minute brainstorming challenge
4	I never follow through.	I'm building discipline step by step.	Complete one small task before noon
5	I don't belong in this space.	I bring a unique and valuable perspective.	Speak up once in a group or meeting
6	I always mess things up.	I learn quickly from mistakes and adjust.	Journal one thing you learned today
7	Success isn't for people like me.	I am being positioned for purpose and success.	Write 3 wins from the past 30 days

Small mindset shifts create massive lifestyle pivots over time.

Activation Questions

1. What are 1–2 default beliefs you've held that might not be true?
2. Where did they come from—an experience, a family narrative, fear?
3. What does Scripture say about who you are, not just what you've done?
4. Whose assumptions are you still trying to live under?
5. What would change if your story was a launching pad, not a label?

Prayer

"God, renew my mind. Show me the false limits I've accepted. Help me flip the script I've been living under

—whether from others or my own fear. Give me the creativity, clarity, and courage to see myself the way You do. In Jesus' name, amen."

Chapter Summary

- Most mental limits aren't real—they're rehearsed
- Innovation starts with asking, *"What else could this be?"*
- Reframing is a spiritual and strategic discipline
- Jesus challenged assumptions to heal, restore, and release people
- You are not too late, too broken, or too small
- Your mind is not a prison—it's a platform

In Chapter 8, we'll explore **Innovation Through Collaboration**—how teaming up with others multiplies insight, dismantles bias, and opens doors that would never open alone.

CHAPTER 8: INNOVATION THROUGH COLLABORATION

"Two are better than one, because they have a good reward for their labor."
— Ecclesiastes 4:9 (NKJV)

From Vision Alone to Vision Together

Some of my greatest breakthroughs didn't come in moments of isolation—they came when I invited other people into the process. There was a time when I thought I had to carry it all. Lead it all. See it all. But when I opened the door to collaboration—something shifted.

One of those shifts happened during the early days of launching City of Light. The vision I carried was big: a multiethnic church in one of the most segregated regions in the country. I had ideas, drive, and a clear sense of mission. But what I didn't have was everything else—like funding, strategy, or local momentum. What made the difference? People.

It was a group of friends, creatives, business owners, and ministry partners who helped co-create the journey. Some helped design visuals. Some offered their businesses as event spaces. Some prayed, while others set up folding chairs and bought snacks. I wasn't just building a church—I was discovering that **collaboration multiplies courage**.

You don't need to have it all figured out. You need to bring what you have—and trust that others will bring what they have. Innovation rarely comes from the lone genius—it's born when different people bring their part of the puzzle.

Real-World Collaboration That Changed Everything

- **Ben & Jerry's** didn't start with a formal business plan. Just two guys—one with a passion for ice cream, the other for funky flavors—deciding to rent an abandoned gas station. Together, they built a brand that became a social movement.

- **The Knowledge House** (NYC) was born from collaboration between tech professionals, educators, and Bronx community leaders. They combined skills and perspectives to give underserved youth access to STEM careers.

- In **Atlanta**, **Jamila Norman**, founder of **Patchwork City Farms**, co-created the **Southwest Atlanta Growers Cooperative (SWAG Coop)**—a network of Black urban farmers committed to sustainable agriculture, food justice, and community empowerment. Together, they've built more than individual farms; they've cultivated food security, created educational programs, and strengthened economic opportunity in underserved neighborhoods.

Their story illustrates that collaboration isn't just about shared resources—it's about shared vision and collective impact.

Innovation is rarely solo. It's relational.

Biblical Collaborations That Changed History:

Moses & Jethro – Collaboration Brings Clarity

In **Exodus 18**, Moses was exhausted from judging every dispute himself. His father-in-law Jethro observed the bottleneck and offered wisdom:

Exodus 18:17–18 (NKJV)

> "So Moses' father-in-law said to him, 'The thing that you do is not good. Both you and these people who are with you will surely wear yourselves out.'"

Jethro's advice led Moses to appoint capable leaders—decentralizing authority and multiplying impact.

Paul & Barnabas – Collaboration Launches Movements

In **Acts 13**, the Holy Spirit spoke to a diverse group of prophets and teachers in Antioch. Among them: Paul and Barnabas. Their collaboration became the first major missionary movement.

Acts 13:2 (NKJV)

> "As they ministered to the Lord and fasted, the Holy Spirit said, 'Now separate to Me Barnabas and Saul for the work to which I have called them.'"

God launches world-changing assignments through relationships, not just individuals.

Collaboration Frameworks for Modern Use

Take a look on the next pages to discover various models to help you form collaborative teams that make a difference.

Triad Teams

Triad Teams are small, diverse groups of three people formed to solve problems, reflect, or innovate. Their strength comes from blending different backgrounds—age, culture, or experience—to unlock fresh insight and build trust.

Three people with complementary strengths:

- A visionary (sees future)
- A builder (structures ideas)
- A bridge (connects people)

Use Triads to:

- Test ideas
- Plan events
- Form advisory boards

Cross-Gen Pods

Cross-Generational Pods bring together people from at least three age groups—typically youth, adults, and elders—to reflect on a shared question or challenge. The diversity of life experience helps surface wisdom, creativity, and blind spots that any single generation might miss.

Use these pods to strengthen teams, spark innovation, or build mutual understanding in families, churches, or businesses.

One teen or Gen Z voice + one adult + one elder. These are ideal for churches, nonprofits, and families looking to bridge generational wisdom with innovation.

Use for:

- Community assessments
- Multi-perspective problem solving

Creative Crews

Creative Crews are small, intentionally diverse groups (3–5 people) gathered around a shared challenge or passion. The key is variety—mixing skillsets, backgrounds, and perspectives to foster unexpected insights and collaborative breakthroughs.

These crews meet regularly to brainstorm, prototype, give feedback, or even co-create projects. Whether you're launching a product, designing an event, or solving a community issue, a Creative Crew helps you move from stuck to sparked.

A photographer, a writer, and a strategist walk into a coffee shop... It's not a joke—it's a content launch team.

Use for:

- Campaign creation
- Online business development
- Social outreach

Collaboration Reflection Table

This tool helps you reflect on recent or ongoing collaborative efforts to evaluate what worked, what didn't, and how you can grow from the experience. Use it after team meetings, joint ventures, or creative sessions to sharpen your awareness and become a stronger, more intuitive collaborator.

Question	Your Thoughts
Who are 2–3 people I could build with?	
What skill do I bring to the table?	
What collaboration style suits me?	(Fast-paced? Long-term? Creative bursts?)
What fears or past wounds affect how I work with others?	

The "Collab Canvas"

The Collab Canvas is a simple yet powerful tool to map out a new or existing collaboration. It helps clarify goals, roles, resources, and expectations to ensure alignment from the start. Use it during team planning, community partnerships, or creative group projects.

Use this tool to map out a new or existing collaboration.

Section	Notes & Planning
Shared Goal	What are we trying to create or change?
Who Brings What	Skills, connections, experience
Potential Friction	Where might we clash or stall?
Communication Rhythms	Weekly calls? Monthly meetups? Text check-ins?
First Micro-Mission	What's one small win we can tackle together?

Don't wait for perfection. Collaborate toward momentum.

Activation Questions

1. Have you been trying to build alone because of past disappointment?
2. Who around you is hungry but underutilized?
3. What's one idea or mission you could invite someone else into this week?
4. Have you prayed for the *right people*—not just any people—to build with?

Prayer

"God, thank You for showing me that I don't have to build alone. Help me to recognize the people You've placed in my life—not as competitors, but as co-creators. Heal any wounds from past collaborations and make room in my heart to dream, serve, and build with others again. In Jesus' name, amen."

Chapter Summary

- Innovation thrives in diversity
- Collaboration multiplies momentum, accountability, and creativity
- God uses teams—Moses and Jethro, Paul and Barnabas, Jesus and the disciples
- Simple frameworks like Triads and Pods make collaboration repeatable
- Your dream is too big to carry alone—and it's not supposed to be

In Chapter 9, we'll bring it all together through the **Dreamer Innovation Blueprint**, a step-by-step guide: transforming dreams, passions and pain points into creative breakthroughs for resilient impact—and lasting joy.

CHAPTER 9:
THE DREAMER INNOVATION BLUEPRINT

"Then the mystery was revealed to Daniel in a night vision. So Daniel blessed the God of heaven."
— Daniel 2:19 (NKJV)

From Revelation to Real-World Impact

Throughout this book, we've explored how creativity, innovation, and entrepreneurial purpose can emerge from unexpected places —pressure, questions, even pain. But now, as we come to the final chapter, we return to where much of it truly begins: **your dreams and visions.**

Not just your long-term aspirations, but the dreams you've literally had in the night.
Not just business goals, but the spontaneous flashes of imagination or insight—what Scripture calls **visions**.

These moments, whether subtle or vivid, can carry more than emotion. They may carry **instruction**.

For me, dreams were never just mysterious mental images. They became **guides**—revealing what I needed to see, pray about, or pursue. Years ago, I began dreaming about people and locations in Southeast Wisconsin. The images were specific. The urgency was real. I saw people crying out for something more—some without hope, some divided by race, religion, or geography. I felt the passion for unity rise within me. And I woke up convinced: I wasn't just dreaming. I was being **called.**

That vision eventually led to the formation of **City of Light Church**, which became more than a ministry—it became a movement of reconciliation, creativity, and cross-cultural impact. And it all started with **God speaking in the language of the night**.

Maybe you've had dreams or visions you dismissed, misunderstood, or forgot altogether. Maybe you've been taught to ignore them or write them off as random. But what if God was speaking—and you were one decoding tool away from clarity?

This chapter is designed to help you **decode the language of dreams and visions**, connect them to real-world purpose, and mobilize them into creative, entrepreneurial, and spiritual breakthroughs.

The D.R.E.A.M.E.R CODE: An Interpretive Model for Action

To make the connection between dreams and strategy clear, I want to introduce a tool called the **D.R.E.A.M.E.R CODE** — a 7-part acronym to help you move from revelation to innovation. If you have gotten this far in the book, you now get to take your night dreams and turn them into daytime strategy.

We will begin by unpacking the 7 steps. Next, we will take a look at some examples to get you ready to leverage this powerful tool. Gaining the ability to decode your life's next steps is within reach.

The D.R.E.A.M.E.R. CODE: An Interpretive Model for Action

Letter	Meaning	Description
D	**Discern the Details**	Identify key elements, emotions, symbols, and settings in the dream.
R	**Recognize the Root**	Consider the origin—fear, faith, stress, or God's prompting.
E	**Explore the Emotions**	What feelings are present? Joy, fear, urgency? Emotions often unlock meaning.
A	**Ask What It Might Mean**	Seek interpretation. What could God, your soul, or your mind be revealing?
M	**Map It to Your Life**	Connect the dream to current challenges, decisions, or relationships.
E	**Engage the Insight**	Start a conversation, journal, or pray about what's been revealed.

R	**Respond with Action**	Take one small step—adjust a habit, reach out, create, or pursue healing.

Example:

D.R.E.A.M.E.R. CODE: Sample Dream Walkthrough

Step	Description
D – Discern the Details	Hallways, closed doors, childhood home setting
R – Recognize the Root	You've been thinking about career transitions and feeling stuck
E – Explore the Emotions	You felt anxious and alone
A – Ask What It Might Mean	This could reflect unresolved fear or forgotten dreams tied to your past
M – Map It to Your Life	Begin journaling about your childhood passions and current roadblocks
E – Engage the Insight	Talk with a mentor or coach about what's resurfacing and why it matters now
R – Respond with Action	Take one step—enroll in a class, update your resume, or revisit a dormant goal

The point of the D.R.E.A.M.E.R CODE is not to make every dream "deep"—but to **train your spiritual and creative mind** to listen for direction and possibility in what others might overlook.

While some dreams are straightforward, many are multi-layered —containing meaning that's symbolic, emotional, strategic, or even spiritual. This next model breaks down the five layers you can explore to uncover deeper insights.

The 7 Layers of Dream Interpretation

A Model for Discerning, Interpreting, and Acting on Your Dreams

Not all dreams are the same. Some are symbolic. Others are emotional, strategic, or even spiritually urgent. The **D.R.E.A.M.E.R. CODE** gives you a **layered lens** to examine a dream more deeply and apply it with purpose.

Think of each step as a question that moves you from mystery to meaning:

D – Discern the Details

- What symbols, images, or themes stood out?
- Were there specific colors, numbers, places, or familiar people?

Tool: Use a trusted biblical or metaphorical dream symbol chart to guide your first impressions.

R – Recognize the Root

- What in your life—emotionally, spiritually, or situationally —might this dream be connected to?
- Was there a recent conflict, a big decision, or a hidden fear?

Prompt: Ask yourself, "What was on my heart or mind this week that might have influenced this?"

E – Explore the Emotions

- What feelings did the dream produce—both during and after?
- Did it bring peace, conviction, urgency, hope, or discomfort?

Insight: Emotions are clues. A sense of joy may confirm calling. Fear might highlight a spiritual battle.

A – Ask What It Might Mean

- Could this be symbolic, instructional, prophetic, or even a warning?
- Does anything in the dream mirror your current journey or future direction?

Prompt: Sometimes God invites us to **interpret with Him**, not apart from Him. Ask, "Lord, what are You trying to show me?"

M – Map It to Scripture

- Are there Bible stories or themes that align with the message of the dream?
- Can the dream be tested and anchored in truth?

Anchor: Scripture is your safety net. It ensures consistency with God's character and voice.

E – Engage the Insight

- What might God be asking you to pray about, prepare for, or discern more deeply?
- Who should you process this with (mentor, leader, or trusted peer)?

Tip: Don't rush to act—sometimes engagement means stillness, journaling, or counsel first.

R – Respond with Action

- What's one intentional step you can take in light of the dream?
- How might you activate the insight practically—in your business, relationships, leadership, or personal growth?

Activation: Write down a short plan or commitment. Obedience turns revelation into transformation.

Encouragement:

Your dreams are not random—they're **personal invitations** from God to reflect, respond, and walk in bold purpose. With the **D.R.E.A.M.E.R. CODE**, you now have a step-by-step structure to guide the journey.

Sometimes, we don't need complexity—we just need a clear next step. If you're new to dream interpretation or want a repeatable process, this simple seven-step **D.R.E.A.M.E.R CODE Interpretive Map** gives you a way to reflect and respond with confidence.

The D.R.E.A.M.E.R CODE Interpretive Map

A simple process to take any dream or vision and walk it into clarity and creative action.

The D.R.E.A.M.E.R. CODE: 7 Layer Interpretive Map
Not all dreams are the same. Some are symbolic. Others are emotional, strategic, or even spiritually urgent. The D.R.E.A.M.E.R. Code gives you a layered lens to examine a dream more deeply and apply it with purpose.

Step	Prompt	Purpose
D – Discern the Details	What symbols, images, or themes stood out? Any colors, numbers, places, or familiar	Use a biblical or metaphorical symbol chart to guide your first impressions.

	people?	
R – Recognize the Root	What emotional, spiritual, or situational theme does this connect to?	Reflect on what was on your heart or mind recently.
E – Explore the Emotions	What did you feel during or after the dream?	Emotion is often a clue to the dream's urgency or direction.
A – Ask What It Might Mean	Is the dream symbolic, prophetic, a warning, or instructional?	Partner with God in interpreting its significance.
M – Map It to Scripture	Are there biblical stories or principles that mirror this dream?	Use Scripture as a filter to ensure clarity and truth.
E – Engage the Insight	What might God be prompting you to pray about or discern further?	Reflect, journal, or seek wise counsel.
R – Respond with Action	What's one step you can take in light of the dream?	Apply what you've received in a practical way.

You can use this tool with:

- Dream journals
- Small group discussions
- Creative brainstorming sessions
- Business vision planning
- Strategic prayer moments

God doesn't waste dreams. We just often waste the interpretation window by ignoring the nudge.

From Dream to Direction: The Innovation Blueprint

So far, we've explored how to listen, interpret, and journal your dreams and visions. Now, we shift into **how to mobilize them**.

Here's a deeper look at a practical tool introduced earlier in this book in order to connect three powerful forces:

- Your **dreams** (supernatural or subconscious insight)
- Your **pain points** (personal or observed problems)
- Your **passions** (gifts, callings, or things that keep you up at night)

Together, these three form a bridge to meaningful innovation.

The Innovation Blueprint

Before any big idea takes off, it needs a blueprint—a clear, yet flexible map that connects your insights, passions, and pain points with real-world opportunities. This exercise helps you organize your most powerful ideas into a framework that can lead to business models, ministry initiatives, or creative projects. You don't need a degree or investor to begin. You just need clarity, consistency, and courage.

Category	Questions to Explore	Example
Dream	What insight, theme, or symbol keeps showing up?	Dreamed about kids being left behind
Pain Point	What challenge breaks your heart or frustrates you?	Local teens lack access to mentors or tech
Passion	What skill, interest, or calling can you contribute?	You love teaching and creating safe spaces
Possible Solution	What idea or experiment could begin solving this?	Launch a weekly coding night at the library

This is the sweet spot where **God-breathed vision** meets **personal**

mission and **real-world application.**

Self-Assessment: Dreamer Innovation Score

Before you build something powerful, it helps to know where you currently stand. This self-assessment is designed to give you a snapshot of your strengths and blind spots when it comes to turning dreams into action.

You'll reflect on areas like:

- Awareness of your passions and pain points
- Willingness to take risks or reframe challenges
- Use of collaboration and creative strategies
- Your current pace of idea execution

There's no "perfect" score—just a clearer picture of your readiness and where to grow next.

After scoring, you'll receive suggestions for which chapters of the *Dreamer Code* to revisit for deeper breakthrough. Think of this as your starting map—because even the boldest dreamers need a compass.

Rate each statement from 1 (not true at all) to 5 (absolutely true):

Statement	Score (1–5)
I consistently remember and write down dreams or creative ideas.	
I reflect on how dreams or insights may relate to my current season.	
I regularly notice patterns in my life that might carry meaning.	
I've taken at least one real-world step based on a dream or vision.	
I can identify a passion or cause that energizes me.	

I've shared a dream or insight with someone I trust for feedback.	
I believe God still speaks through dreams, visions, and impressions.	
I have a rhythm of journaling, planning, or praying into my insights.	

Total Score:

35–40: Dreamer in Motion

You're tuned in and actively walking in vision.
To stay sharp, revisit:

- **Chapter 6** (*Unlocking Innovation Through Questions*)
- **Chapter 8** (*Innovation Through Collaboration*) — to multiply your efforts with others

25–34: Dreamer in Training

You're listening, now take bolder steps.
To grow, re-read:

- **Chapter 2** (*The Power of Perception*) — to sharpen your ability to observe and connect
- **Chapter 4** (*Mapping Dreams, Pain, and Passion*) — to link your insights to specific action
- **Chapter 5** (*Dream Symbols & Real World Problems*) — to gain deeper interpretive skill

15–24: Dreamer on Pause

Your inner vision may be dimmed by distraction or

discouragement.

To reawaken clarity and boldness, start with:

- **Chapter 3** (*Awareness*) — to re-engage your attention and discernment

- **Chapter 7** (*Breaking Mental Limits*) — to challenge your assumptions and move forward

Below 15: Dreamer Reawakening

You may have silenced your creative or spiritual voice—but it's not too late.

Begin again with:

- **Chapter 1** (*The Sons of Issachar*) — to understand your times and start seeing purpose again

- **Chapter 9** (*This chapter*) — to rebuild your rhythm and receive permission to dream again

Final Activation Questions

1. What's one dream, vision, or persistent idea you've been ignoring?
2. What pain point keeps reappearing in your environment or community?
3. Which part of the D.R.E.A.M.E.R Code do you need to practice more?
4. What's one small step you can take in the next 7 days?

Final Prayer

"God, thank You for speaking to me in ways both quiet and bold. Open my eyes to what You're revealing—through dreams, visions, longings, and even discomfort. Help me interpret with wisdom, act with courage, and build with creativity. Let what You've shown me become a gift I release to the world. In Jesus' name, amen."

A Word Before You Go

If this book stirred something inside you—questions, hope, conviction, or new ideas—I want you to know: **you're not alone.**

What started as a spark can become a strategy. What began in a journal can become a movement. This is not the end of your innovation journey—it's only the beginning.

To continue this conversation, join me in upcoming episodes of the **Dreamer's Blueprint Podcast**—where we'll explore practical tools, hear from other creatives and visionaries, and keep learning how to turn revelation into real impact.

Final Thought

You were made to have dreams and visions—you were made to build what they show you.
Let your dreams and visions speak.
Let your creativity flow.
And let your life become the blueprint someone else needs in the challenging times we face in the world today.

Books & Resources That Inspired This Work

Dream Science & Psychology

- Walker, Matthew. *Why We Sleep: Unlocking the Power of Sleep and Dreams*. Scribner, 2017.
- Barrett, Deirdre. *The Committee of Sleep: How Artists, Scientists, and Athletes Use Dreams for Creative Problem Solving*. Oneiroi Press, 2001.
- Hobson, J. Allan. *Dreaming: An Introduction to the Science of Sleep*. Oxford University Press, 2002.

Biblical & Prophetic Insight

- Simmons, Brian. *The Passion Translation Bible: Dreams & Interpretation Footnotes*. BroadStreet Publishing.
- Sandford, John & Paula. *The Elijah Task: A Call to Today's Prophets*. Charisma House, 2006.
- Cain, Herman Riffel. *Dream Interpretation: A Biblical Understanding*. Destiny Image, 2000.

Innovation & Creativity

- Johnson, Steven. *Where Good Ideas Come From: The Natural History of Innovation*. Riverhead Books, 2010.
- Kelley, Tom & Kelley, David. *Creative Confidence: Unleashing the Creative Potential Within Us All*. Crown Business, 2013.
- Tharp, Twyla. *The Creative Habit: Learn It and Use It for Life*. Simon & Schuster, 2003.

Statistics & Cultural Data

- Pew Research Center. *Religious Landscape Study: Religious Belief and Practices*. Pew Forum, 2009.
- YouGov. *Dreams and Nightmares Study*. YouGov America, 2018.
- Harvard Medical School. *Division of Sleep Medicine: Understanding Sleep*. hms.harvard.edu.

ABOUT THE AUTHOR

Brian D Mckee

Brian D. McKee is a visionary, innovation strategist, pastor and seasoned cybersecurity professional. With over a decade of experience helping individuals and organizations navigate change. Brian combines spiritual insight with cutting-edge problem-solving. He leads a thriving, multiethnic church in one of the most highly segregated areas of the United States and has helped grow it to over 400 members in 9 years.

Brian has hosted AI training events, economic empowerment hackathons, and launched creative business incubators that bridge urban and suburban communities. His passion for dream interpretation, prophetic insight, and entrepreneurship fuels his mission to help others unlock the God-given ideas within them. Through Dreamer Code, Brian empowers readers to merge vision with innovation and turn dreams into transformative action.